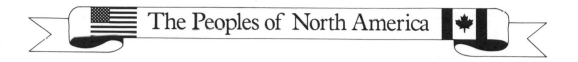

THE JAPANESE AMERICANS

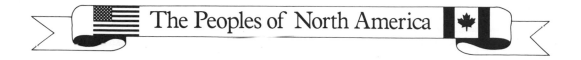
The Peoples of North America

THE JAPANESE
AMERICANS

Harry Kitano

CHELSEA HOUSE PUBLISHERS
New York • New Haven • Philadelphia

Library of Congress Cataloging-in-Publication Data

Kitano, Harry H. L.
   The Japanese Americans.
   (The Peoples of North America)
   Includes index.
   Summary: Discusses the history, culture, and religion of the Japanese, factors encouraging their emigration, and their acceptance as an ethnic group in North America.

   1. Japanese Americans.   [1. Japanese Americans]
   I. Title.   II. Series.
   E184.J3K498   1987   973'.04956   86-28365

   ISBN 0-87754-856-0

Project Editor: Patricia Chambers
Text Editor: Mary Ann Hunsche
Chief Copy Editor: Melissa R. Padovani
Art Director: Maureen McCafferty
Series Designer: Anita Noble
Project Coordinator: Kathleen P. Luczak
Production Manager: Brian A. Shulik

Cover Illustration by Jack Freas. The cover art depicts the heritage of Japanese Americans combined with images of their experiences in North America.

ACKNOWLEDGMENTS

The author and publisher are grateful to these individuals and organizations for information and photographs: The Balch Institute, Philadelphia; Embassy of Japan; Tod Fujihara; George Imai, Japanese Canadian Citizens Association, Toronto, Canada; Japanese National Tourist Organization; George Kiriyama of the Japanese Historical Society of Southern California; Library of Congress for photographs by Clem Albers and Charles Mace; Corky Lee; National Archives; New York Convention and Visitors Bureau; New York City Public Library Picture Collection; Yuichiro Oka, Philadelphia; California State Library, San Francisco, for the photograph on page 28, a gift of Hamilton H. Dobbin. Picture reseach: PAR/NYC.

Contents

A Nation of Nations

Senator Daniel Patrick Moynihan

The Constitution of the United States begins: "We the People of the United States ..." Yet, as we know, the United States is not made up of a single group of people. It is made up of many peoples. Immigrants from Europe, Asia, Africa, South America, Antarctica, and Australia settled in North America seeking a new life filled with opportunities unavailable in their homeland. Coming from many nations, they forged one nation and made it their own. More than 100 years ago, Walt Whitman expressed this perception of America as a melting pot: "Here is not merely a nation, but a teeming Nation of nations."

It was the ingenuity and acts of courage of these immigrants, our ancestors, that shaped the North American way of life. Yet, we sometimes take their contributions for granted. This fine series, *The Peoples of North America*, examines the experiences and contributions of the immigrants and how these contributions determined the future of the United States, Canada, and Mexico.

The immigrants did not abandon their ethnic traditions when they reached the shores of North America. Each ethnic group had its own customs and traditions, and each brought different experiences, accomplishments, skills, values, styles of dress, and tastes in food that lingered long after its arrival. Yet this profusion of differences created a singularity, or bond, among the immigrants. The poet Robert Frost put it well: "The land was ours before we were the land's."

The United States and Canada are unique in this respect. Whereas religious and ethnic differences sparked wars throughout the rest of the world—from the 17th-century religious wars to the 19th-century nationalist movements in Europe to the near extermination of the Jews under Nazi Germany—*we* learned to respect each other's differences and to live as one.

And the differences were as varied as the millions of immigrants who sought a new life in North America. In a mass migration, some 12 million immigrants passed through the waiting rooms of New York's Ellis Island; thousands more came to the West Coast. At first, these immigrants were welcomed because labor was needed to meet the demands of the Industrial Age. Soon, however, the new immigrants faced the prejudice of earlier immigrants who saw them as a burden on the economy. Legislation was passed to limit immigration. The Chinese Exclusion Act of 1882 was among the first laws closing the doors to the promise of America. The Japanese were also effectively excluded by this law. In 1924, Congress established immigration quotas on a country-by-country basis.

Such prejudices might have erupted into war, as they did in Europe, but North Americans chose negotiation and compromise, instead. This determination to resolve differences peacefully has been the hallmark of the countries of North America.

The unique ability of Americans to live together as one people was seriously threatened by the issue of slavery. It was a symptom of a growing attitude of intolerance in the world. Thousands of English settlers had arrived in the colonies as indentured servants. These Englishmen agreed to work for a specified number of years on a farm or as a craftsman's apprentice in return for passage to America and room and board. When the first Africans arrived in the then-British colonies during the 17th century, some colonists thought that they should be treated as indentured servants, too. Eventually, the question of whether the Africans should be considered indentured, like the Englishmen, or slaves who could be owned for life was considered in a Maryland court. The court's calamitous decree held that blacks were slaves bound to lifelong servitude, and so were their children. America went through a time of moral examination and civil war pitting brother against brother before it finally freed African slaves, as well as their descendants. The principle that all men are created equal had faced its greatest challenge and survived.

The court ruling that set blacks apart from other races fanned flames of discrimination that lasted long after slavery was abolished. The concept of racism had existed for centuries in countries throughout the world. When the Manchus conquered China in the 13th century, they decreed that Chinese and Manchus could not intermarry. To impress their superiority on the conquered Chinese, the Manchus ordered all Chinese men to wear their hair in a long braid called a queue.

By the 19th century, some intellectuals took up the banner of racism, citing Charles Darwin's work on the evolution of animals as proof of their position. Darwin's studies theorized that highly evolved animals were dominant over other animals. Some advocates of this theory applied it to humans, asserting that certain races were more highly evolved than others and thus were superior.

This philosophy served as the basis for a new discrimination, not only against certain races, but also against various ethnic groups. These ugly ideas were directed at black people and other victims as well. Asians faced harsh discrimination and were depicted by 19th-century newspaper cartoonists who chronicled public opinion as depraved, degenerate people, deficient in intelligence. When the Irish flooded American cities to escape the famine in Ireland, the cartoonists caricatured the typical "Paddy" (a popular term for Irish immigrants) as an apelike creature with jutting jaw and sloping forehead.

By the 20th century, these concepts of racism and ethnic prejudice had developed into virulent theories of a Northern European master race. When Adolf Hitler came to power in Germany in 1933, he popularized the notion of Aryan supremacy. "Aryan," a term referring to the Indo-European races, was applied to so-called superior physical characteristics such as blond hair, blue eyes, and delicate facial features. Anyone with darker and heavier features was considered inferior. Based upon these theories, the German Nazi state from 1933 to 1945 set out to destroy European Jews, along with Gypsies and other groups considered inferior. It nearly succeeded. Millions of these people were killed.

How supremely important it is, then, that we have learned to live with one another, respecting differences while treasuring the things we share.

A relatively recent example of this nonviolent way of resolving differences is the solution the Canadians found to a conflict between two ethnic groups. The conflict arose in the mid-1960s between the peoples of French-speaking Quebec Province and those of the English-speaking provinces. Relations grew tense, then bitter, then violent. The Royal Commission on Bilingualism and Biculturalism was established to study the growing crisis and to propose measures to ease the tensions. As a result of the commission's recommendations, all official documents and statements from the national government's capital at Ottawa are now issued in both French and English, and bilingual education is encouraged.

The year 1980 marked a coming of age for the United States' ethnic heritage. For the first time, the U.S. Census asked people about their ethnic background. Americans chose from more than 100 groups, including French Basque, Spanish Basque, French Canadian, Afro-American, Peruvian, Armenian, Chinese, and Japanese, among others. The ethnic group with the largest response was English (49.6 million). More than 100 million Americans claimed ancestors from the British Isles, which includes Ireland, Wales, and Scotland. There were almost as many Germans (49.2 million) as English. The Irish-American population (40.2) was third, but the next largest ethnic group, the Afro-Americans, was a distant fourth (21 million). There was a sizable group of French ancestry (13 million), as well as Italian (12 million). Poles, Dutch, Swedes, Norwegians and Russians followed. These groups, and other smaller ones, represent the wondrous profusion of ethnic influences in North America.

Canada, too, has discovered the diversity of its population. Studies conducted during the French/English conflict determined that Canadians were descended from Ukrainians, Germans, Italians, Chinese, Japanese, native Indians, and Eskimos. Canada found it had no ethnic majority, although nearly half of its immigrant population came from the British Isles. Canada, like the United States, is a land of immigrants for whom mutual tolerance is a matter of reason as well as principle. Tolerance is a virtue that has brought North America peace.

The people of North America are the descendants of one of the greatest migrations in history. That migration is not over. Koreans, Vietnamese, Nicaraguans, and Cubans are heading for the shores of North America in large numbers. This mix of cultures shapes every aspect of our lives. To understand ourselves, we must know something about our ethnic ancestry as well as the ancestry of others, because in a sense, they are part of our history, too. Nothing so defines the North American nations as the motto on the Great Seal of the United States: *E Pluribus Unum*—Out of Many, One.

Endurance and Acceptance

Few ethnic cultures have been as thoroughly accepted by American society as the Japanese. Americans drive Japanese cars, eat sushi, collect Japanese prints, and study the martial arts.

Acceptance did not come easily for Japanese Americans. But the ancient Japanese traditions of endurance and acceptance of fate helped them wait patiently for it. The bases of these traditional beliefs were the religions of Japan—Shinto, Buddhism, and Christianity. Although Japan was controlled by leaders who fought bloody battles for domination, the Japanese religions taught the importance of harmony, cooperation, and acceptance. For the Japanese, acceptance of the hand that fate has dealt is a longstanding tradition rooted in their religion and their history.

Throughout the past century, the acceptance of Japanese Americans has depended upon the relationship between the Western powers and Japan, and that relationship has swung from one extreme to another.

13

■ *European trading activities became a popular subject for Japanese artists, as illustrated by this 18th-century screen.*

By the time the West established trade with Japan, the Japanese had endured more than 300 years of feudal wars and become a police state controlled by *shoguns,* or military dictators. The shoguns restricted all contact with the outside world for more than 250 years. Finally in 1867, the Emperor Meiji ended that enforced isolation. Meiji permitted Westerners to trade in Japan and borrowed European and American technology to bring his rural, isolated nation to the status of a world power within a generation.

When Japan opened its doors to the West, it revealed artistic treasures hidden from Western eyes for 250 years. Japanese art was inspired by Buddhism, a religion that used nature's inherent balance as a model for the idyllic life. When this art was unveiled in the West, it created a revolution in artistic form. Japan's 17th century *Ukiyo-e* ("pictures of the floating world") strongly influenced French and American lithographers and impressionist painters of the 19th century. These pictures, made from meticulously crafted

14

woodblocks, were printed in black ink and then hand-colored in vivid hues. This technique inspired the modern poster and was an important influence on French painter Henri de Toulouse-Lautrec. It also led to the development of silk-screen art.

When the Japanese immigrants arrived in North America in the late 1860s, they were not welcomed as readily as Japanese artforms had been. American industrialists, anxious for a new source of labor, had invited the Japanese to immigrate. When the Japanese did come to North America, however, suspicion greeted them. This suspicion was sparked by fear that Japan's new military power threatened Western nations.

The Japanese were not the only immigrants to face prejudice in their new land. For more than two decades, the Chinese had come in great num-

Japanese woodcuts such as this one inspired the development of silk-screen and modern poster art.

Foreigners in foreign clothing poured into Japan, as depicted by this 17th-century Ukiyo-e.

bers to work in Hawaii, Canada, and the American mainland. Their native country, however, had been defeated by Western powers eager to profit from trade with China. Therefore, the Japanese immigration seemed more threatening. In America, the Japanese faced the same prejudice and legal restrictions as the Chinese, but they found more ways to work within the restrictions. They were not discouraged by failures. Their religion and the bloody political struggles of their homeland had taught them that a just man succeeds in the end.

The suspicion and anti-Asian sentiment against the Japanese Americans exploded on December 7, 1941, when Japanese forces attacked the United States Naval Fleet at Pearl Harbor. Japanese Americans took the brunt of anti-Asian prejudice that had smoldered in America for decades.

Japanese Americans were labeled "enemy aliens," evacuated from their homes, and held in detention camps in the United States from 1942 to 1945. Canada took similar measures. More than 110,000 Japanese Americans were imprisoned despite the fact that most of them were American citizens. Japanese Americans found their dream of a better life in the New World—the dream of all immigrants—shattered.

When the war ended, Japanese Americans left the detention camps to rebuild their lives. Their traditional beliefs, which emphasized endurance and a strong sense that all things work together for the common good, gave them the strength to look to the future.

Religion and Politics

Religion and historical events played important roles in developing the Japanese character. Japan's early religions deified the emperor and stressed that all things worked together for the common good. As a result, no matter how oppressive the ruling lords became, the Japanese people believed that fate guided their path through life. Endurance, patience, and acceptance became cherished virtues.

As each of Japan's three main religions—Shinto, Buddhism, and Christianity—was introduced, the Japanese lifestyle changed to incorporate the new practices and beliefs. None of the old religious practices disappeared. Japanese families commonly kept both a Shinto shrine and a Buddhist altar.

Shinto was the religion of Japan during the reign of Empress Jingo in the 4th century. A warrior empress, Jingo expanded the boundaries of Japan and incorporated many Chinese influences, including Shinto, into its culture. This religion emphasized strong family ties

19

and ancestor worship. Each family had its own shrine, dedicated to the *kami*, or spirit of an ancestor.

In 552 A.D., the Chinese influence brought another religion, Buddhism, to Japan. Buddhism stressed a ritual sense of order with the goal of inner peace. It anchored itself in the precept that the only universal law was one of constant change. This religion encouraged the individual to obey the guidance of his own inner light.

In China, Buddhism was closely tied to the teachings of the prophet Confucius. When Buddhism was imported to Japan, the Confucian influence came with it. Confucianism taught that a nation should model itself on the social order of the family and stressed respect for authority. These ideas blended comfortably with Shinto.

This wooden sculpture is a tribute to Japan's Empress Jingo.

 *Natural elements and human creativity merge in this rock and sand garden, which decorates the grounds at Myoshiji Temple in Kyoto.*

 *Visitors to this Shinto temple purify themselves before entering.*

21

Prince Shōtoku (center) reorganized the government according to Buddhist and Confucian philosophies.

Among the early, enthusiastic students of Buddhism was Prince Shōtoku (573-621 A.D.). Although he practiced Buddhism, Shōtoku was fascinated by Confucianism. He combined the philosophy of this Chinese prophet and Buddhism to reorganize the government. Following the Confucian code of behavior, Shōtoku proclaimed a set of 17 principles for the Japanese people. The principles stressed the Buddhist philosophy of harmony. They also proclaimed that the "will of heaven" took precedence over the power of any ruler.

Emperors and nobles embraced Buddhism, and by the early 7th century, it was the official religion of Japan. Members of the Japanese imperial court built elaborate Buddhist temples and monasteries. Buddhist monks became counselors to the shoguns, and their monasteries became important centers of learning and commerce.

The Buddhist influence reached its peak during the 15th century, when Ashikaga shoguns used Buddhist monks as warriors. From the end of the 12th century until the early 17th century, battling clans kept Japan in an almost constant state of war. By controlling the monks' military power, the shoguns became dictators while the emperors, enthralled with the Buddhist concept of Nirvana (the blissful state), chose to withdraw into a lavish, contemplative haven away from the people.

While the shoguns ruled Japan, two military classes developed. The *daimyo* were feudal lords under the authority of the shoguns. They were protected by a warrior class called the *samurai.* The emperors collected high taxes to support the court's lavish lifestyle but exempted the feudal lords from the taxes to ensure their loyalty. This system left the peasants to carry most of the tax burden. Eventually, high taxes forced the peasants to surrender their land to the feudal lords.

As the feudal lords struggled for domination, Oda Nobunaga (1534-1582) emerged as a strong, yet cruel, leader of the divergent Japanese people. The motto inscribed on his personal seal was "to bring the whole country under one sword." To accomplish this goal, Nobunaga first turned to the Buddhist warriors. Soon, however, he began to distrust them. When Christian missionaries arrived in Japan in 1549, Nobunaga saw a chance to end

This samurai was one of the warriors who supported Japan's military dictators, the shoguns.

the power of the Buddhist monks. Through the missionaries, Nobunaga met Portuguese traders who offered him a new weapon—firearms. He used these new weapons to defeat the Buddhists. Nobunaga's most infamous act was the destruction of the 800-year-old Buddhist monastery at Mt. Hiei. In the name of law and order, he destroyed more than 3,000 buildings at the monastery and killed its 20,000 inmates.

With his new power, Nobunaga sent armies to conquer the territory surrounding Japan. He died at the hands of one his own generals before he could achieve his goal. One of his followers, Hideyoshi (1536-1598), succeeded him. Hideyoshi gained a reputation for being gracious toward friends and foes alike, but did not abandon Nobunaga's dream of conquering East Asia. He strengthened the Japanese navy and sent expeditions in 1592 and

◲ *The many Buddhist shrines that grace Japan's landscape pay tribute to a religion that has helped shape the country for nearly 1500 years.*

1597 to challenge the Chinese. To maintain peace among the feudal lords, Hideyoshi adhered to the traditional organization of Japanese society, favoring the old military aristocracy. He took many steps to protect this aristocracy, such as prohibiting the Japanese peasants from changing jobs or residence and allowing only samurai to carry weapons.

In 1588, Hideyoshi announced that swords would be collected from everyone but samurai. He claimed the action was being taken to build a Great Buddha image:

> Swords and short swords thus collected will not be wasted. They shall be used as nails and bolts in the construction of the Great Image of Buddha. This will benefit the people not only in this life but also in the life hereafter.

Hideyoshi spent much of his great wealth building a Great Buddha image in Kyoto. Although he continued his attacks on Buddhist monasteries, Hideyoshi's public support of Buddhism enabled him to use religion to control the Japanese people and to enforce strict codes of conduct governing every aspect of life.

Eventually, Hideyoshi and the Ashikaga shoguns were overthrown by another follower of Nobunaga, Ieyasu (1542-1616), who created the Tokugawa shogunate in 1615. The Tokugawa shoguns became powerful by enforcing Confucian principles that stressed a strict behavioral code. Ritual became so important that even the proper way to drink tea was defined by ceremony.

Christianity: A Western Influence

Christianity brought the influence of Europe and America to Japan. This new religion worried the Tokugawa shoguns, who believed the Western nations were using Christianity to fool the Japanese into accepting passive conquest. The Western nations had fought a series of trade wars against the Chinese government, and the Tokugawa shoguns were determined to prevent the Western nations from taking over Japan as they had China.

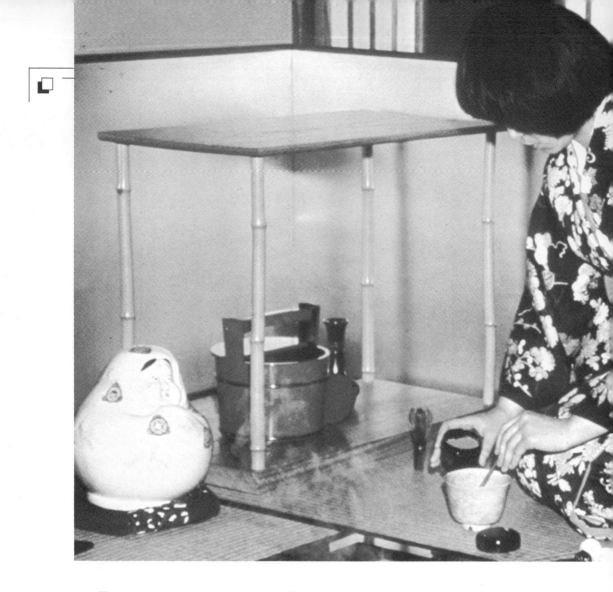

To counter this new threat, the Tokugawa shoguns persecuted Christians. Their stringent measures against Christian influences effectively closed off Japan from the Western world. They barred Christian missionaries and other Westerners until the end of the Tokugawa period in 1867.

Christianity itself did not have a serious impact on Japanese culture, but its introduction brought drastic changes to Japanese society. Strict laws forbade the Japanese from leaving Japan or having any contact with Westerners. The Japanese peasants knew survival depended upon accepting the authority of each new shogun without question. Although Japanese had traveled as far as Siam, the Philippines, and Singapore before the Tokugawa period, the policies of the Tokugawa shoguns meant that a Japanese citizen

□ *This Geisha performs the Japanese Tea Ceremony, which is based on ancient codes of behavior.*

who left for the West could not return. The laws even forbade the construction of large ships to prevent Japanese emigration.

By the mid-1800s, the Western powers were anxious to open trade routes to Japan to take advantage of Japan's lucrative silk industry. They also were eager to find new workers for the Hawaiian sugar cane plantations. To achieve their goals, they joined forces with the Japanese lord Mutsuhito to defeat the Tokugawa shogunate. When they succeeded, the doors to Japan opened for the first time in 250 years.

These political changes made little difference in the lives of the Japanese peasants. But their new freedom to emigrate to America meant opportunities beyond anything possible in Japan.

教會廣告

四月十二日（水）午后七時
主題矯風会。
　　　　　　祈禱会

四月十五日（日）午前九時半
日曜學校聖書研究（英日）
禮拜説教　十二川十時半
「服従ノ報酬」
英語集会　午后七時半
　　　　ミス・ワーレン・

日本人紅會

BY PERMISSION OF BOARD OF HARBOR COM—.

Opening the Doors to the West

Emperor Mutsuhito defeated the Tokugawa shoguns with the help of Western nations vying for control of the lucrative Japanese trade. He took the name Meiji, meaning "enlightened government," and was determined to make his island nation a world power.

During the struggle between Mutsuhito and the shoguns in the 1860s, American emissaries arrived in Japan officially to negotiate the release of American whalers stranded by shipwrecks. Actually, the American emissaries were trying to obtain trade agreements. When Mutsuhito took power, he negotiated agreements with the United States and Great Britain, giving the two nations the first access to Japanese trade in 15 generations.

It was during Mutsuhito's reign that Japanese began immigrating to the United States, first to Hawaii and later to the American mainland. The first Japanese emigrants went to Hawaii in 1868 to work on the sugar cane plantations. These emigrants, mostly illiterate city

PHOTO COURTESY BISHOP MUSEUM

■ *The emperor Meiji, portrayed here in military garb, ended the restriction on Japanese emigration.*

PHOTO COURTESY BISHOP MUSEUM

■ *Many Japanese went to work in Hawaii's pineapple fields.*

dwellers from Yamaguchi and Hiroshima, so identified with the Japanese government that they called themselves *Gan-nen-mono,* "first year men," referring to the first year of the Meiji reign.

The Japanese workers came to Hawaii under three-year contracts, but life on the sugar plantations was harsh. Some Japanese, resenting cruel treatment from plantation owners and overseers, complained to their government about the *haole* (landlords). In response, the Japanese government sent an ambassador to ensure fair treatment for its citizens. After negotiating with the labor contractors, Japan's ambassador arranged for 60 of the original immigrant workers to return home. The situation created so much tension between Japan and Hawaii that 17 years passed before another immigrant ship sailed to the Hawaiian Islands.

Although the work was hard and many of them were city residents unaccustomed to field work, most of these first Japanese immigrants stayed in Hawaii when their three-year contract expired. Despite the hardships,

these immigrants saw a chance to escape the strict class limitations and increasing militarism of Japan.

By the turn of the century, Japanese labor was in great demand in Hawaii. Chinese labor had been excluded from the United States in 1888, so American industry turned to Japan as a source of inexpensive labor. Japan cooperated by screening its emigrants for good character, which made them even more attractive to the plantation owners. By 1899, more than 65,000 Japanese workers had immigrated to Hawaii.

Gradually, conditions began to change for the plantation owners as the courts, pressured by the growing American labor movement, began to protect workers from harsh treatment. When Hawaii was annexed as a United States territory in 1898, politicians on the mainland began scrutinizing working conditions on the plantations.

President Theodore Roosevelt (1858-1919) strongly objected to the discrimination and poor working conditions Asians faced. In December 1905, he made a speech making his position known:

> The status of servility can never again be tolerated on American soil. No merely half-hearted effort to meet its problems as other American communities have met theirs can be accepted as final. Hawaii shall never become a territory in which a governing class of rich planters exist by means of coolie labor.

Within two years, however, Roosevelt bowed to public pressure and negotiated a quota system, called the Gentlemen's Agreement, to limit immigration from Japan. Canada established a similar agreement in response to pressure from laborers there who feared the Japanese would take their jobs by working for lower wages. Conditions began to change in 1888 when American law halted Chinese immigration. By the early 1900s, Japanese laborers were confident enough of their dominance in the labor market to test it with strikes in 1909 and 1920.

Eventually, the Japanese laborers' wages increased, and the added income encouraged many of them to seek a better life by opening their own businesses and practicing trades. By the 1940s, Japanese accounted for 40

(continued on page 41)

Immigrants' Album

Japanese immigrants introduced Americans to sushi—a dinner that combines flavor and beauty.

■ *Hawaiian Japanese built a temple, modeled on a temple in Japan, to commemorate immigration.*

■ *A woman in traditional dress demonstrates an ancient Japanese instrument, the samisen.*

The drama of Japanese kabuki theater.

Pottery such as this 4th-century vase shows Japan's history of artistic achievement.

A Japanese New Year's celebration.

Carp flags fly to celebrate the Japanese Boys' Day festival.

Many Japanese worshipped at this Buddhist shrine, which dates from the Nara period.

Ikebana, the art of Japanese flower arranging, is popular in America.

■ *People line the streets of Los Angeles to watch the Nisei Week Parade.*

■ *The first step in the voyage to America is depicted in this 19th-century photo.*

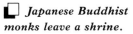 *Japanese Buddhist monks leave a shrine.*

 *This painting depicts sugar plantation laborers.*

Americans learn the Japanese martial art of judo.

This Shinto cemetery in Japan is dotted with clay sculptures.

This Shinto Temple in Hawaii was modeled on Japan's Heian shrine.

Field workers changed into traditional kimonos after a day's work.

PHOTO COURTESY BISHOP MUSEUM

(continued from page 32)

percent of the merchants in Hawaii. Many Japanese men became carpenters, and some Japanese women became barbers.

The Japanese Arrive in California

In 1890, only 2,039 Japanese lived on the North American mainland, but by 1920, they numbered more than 111,000. Some 40,000 of these immigrants had lived in Hawaii before they traveled to the mainland. The majority of these new immigrants, however, were impoverished farmers from Japan's southern provinces.

Most of the Japanese immigrants came to the United States during a period of a few years—1890 to 1907. There were fewer Japanese immigrants than most other ethnic groups: less than 1 percent of the total immigrant population, or about 271,000 people. At the turn of the century nearly 80 percent of all Japanese immigrants to America were living in California. Perhaps because of this strongly clustered settlement, the Japanese found themselves the brunt of anti-Asian sentiment that had built up since the great influx of Chinese workers at the turn of the 19th century.

Because of legal restrictions, Japanese owned only about 4 percent of California's farmland, but they produced more than 10 percent of the state's

41

■ *In 1900, Japanese immigrants who had fulfilled their field labor contracts owned and operated most barbershops in Honolulu.*

farm crops. They were the first to make rice-growing a profitable venture in California. They converted swamps or arid land into productive farms and offered new products such as flowers, celery, and strawberries. Ironically, their very success fueled anti-Asian sentiments.

A provision set by the First United States Congress in 1790 declaring that only free, white persons were eligible for citizenship was used to prevent Chinese from becoming naturalized citizens of the United States. When the Japanese immigrated, this legal tactic was also applied to them.

From the time that the Gentlemen's Agreement between Japan and the United States took effect until several years after World War II, the Califor-

42

nia legislature introduced anti-Japanese legislation at each session. In 1924, the United States government bowed to pressure by anti-Asian groups and passed an immigration act making aliens ineligible for citizenship. Fearing they would not be able to return to America if they traveled to Japan, those Japanese who had established families and businesses in America felt trapped. They were unable to become citizens of their new country and unable to return to their native country. Prejudice was so strong that Japanese-born immigrants could not become naturalized American citizens until 1952.

"Yellow Peril" Politics

As Japanese continued to immigrate to America, events in their homeland fueled anti-Asian sentiment in America. Emperor Meiji, who ruled until 1912, did much more than open emigration from and European trade with Japan. Determined to prevent the Western powers from taking over Japan as they had neighboring China, he completely reorganized the Japanese political structure and society by incorporating specific Western influences.

He hired French officers to restructure the army, British seamen to reorganize the navy, and Dutch engineers to oversee construction throughout Japan. He sent emissaries to the United States and Europe to discover which programs could best be duplicated in Japan. He instituted a new penal code, modeled on that of France, and developed a ministry of education based upon the United States' educational system. Meiji modeled the government cabinet on the German system and declared universal military service in 1872. Then, in 1876, he abolished the samurai class.

Immigrants in California opened this nursery before World War II.

With these innovations accomplished, Meiji began to expand Japan's power. Japan fought and soundly defeated China during the Sino-Japanese War of 1894 to 1895, taking control of Taiwan and the Pescadores islands. The Treaty of Shimonoseki that ended the Sino-Japanese War in 1895 would have awarded the Liaodong Peninsula (southern Manchuria) to Japan, but political pressure from Russia, France, and Germany prevented this provision. This disagreement eventually led Japan into war with Russia from 1904 to 1905.

Russia had leased Port Arthur from China in 1898 as a headquarters for its navy in the Pacific and sent troops into Manchuria to strengthen this

Japanese troops march through an occupied Chinese village during the Sino-Japanese War. Meiji's attempt to extend Japan's power was successful.

Schoolchildren are drilled in military tactics as Japan prepares for warfare.

position. Trouble developed, however, when Russia refused to recognize Japan's interests in Korea. Japan blockaded the Russian fleet at Port Arthur on February 8, 1904. Through the mediation of President Theodore Roosevelt, the two nations signed a treaty in which Russia agreed to recognize Japanese control of Korea and to evacuate Manchuria.

Japan's appetite for domination threatened the Western powers and fostered suspicion of the Japanese immigrating to North America. Politicians and journalists, especially the Hearst and McClatchy newspapers, stirred suspicion by claiming that Japan was using its emigrants to prepare a secret attack on the United States. The newspapers called this potential threat the "Yellow Peril" and called for legislation to curb Japanese immigration. Outrageous rumors—such as a story that the Japanese sprayed vegetables with arsenic to poison their customers—fanned anti-Japanese sentiment. 45

By 1905, some 90,000 Japanese had arrived on the West Coast. Labor leaders and politicians vocalized their opposition. San Francisco Mayor James D. Phelan stated his objections to the influx of Japanese laborers:

> The Japanese are starting the same tide of immigration that we thought we had checked twenty years ago.... The Chinese and Japanese are not bona fide citizens. They are not the stuff of which American citizens can be made.... Personally we have nothing against the Japanese, but as they will not assimilate with us and their social life is so different from ours, let them keep at a respectful distance.

Picture Brides

Japanese men greatly outnumbered Japanese women in America. Of the 214,000 Japanese immigrants who arrived in the United States between 1900 and 1920, fewer than 30,000 were women. Prejudice against Asians, including laws forbidding intermarriage between races, meant that the Japanese had to find a way to bring Japanese women to America. Following the Japanese tradition of arranged marriages, the men found a solution in "picture brides."

Japanese men sent their pictures to matchmakers in Japan who arranged marriages through the women's families. These arranged marriages enabled the Japanese to begin families and create American communities. This Japanese innovation was met with suspicion and attacked by politicians and

Japanese men in Hawaii sent home for brides instead of marrying more modern, Hawaiian women.

newspapers. The campaign against picture brides by the McClatchy newspapers persuaded the Japanese government to stop issuing passports to picture brides in 1920.

When the picture brides arrived, many found that their grooms were much older than they appeared in their pictures. When these couples began their families, the husbands were an average age of 38. The age difference created a wide gap between fathers and children. The Japanese immigrants saw themselves as separate them from their children and established specific divisions between the generations—*Issei, Nisei,* and *Sansei.* The Japanese still use these terms to differentiate between the generations.

Issei, Nisei, and Sansei

The Issei were born in Japan and arrived in the United States between 1890 and 1924. The Nisei, American-born children of the Issei, were born

Issei, the first Japanese immigrants to the United States, settled comfortably into their new way of life.

between 1900 and 1940. The Sansei, the third generation, are the Nisei's children. The three terms indicate more than mere age differences. The experiences of each of the three groups resulted in different values, expectations, attitudes, and behavior.

The Issei grew up in Japan. They were products of the Meiji Era, which emphasized values such as obligation, conformity, and loyalty. When immigration ended, the Issei were left isolated from their homeland. Most had a limited knowledge of English and found communication with their American-born children difficult.

Their parents' background and culture influenced the American-born and -educated Nisei, but American culture was also a strong influence. The Sansei and later generations have shared a totally American experience, little influenced by their Japanese heritage.

The majority of Issei were ambitious and intelligent young men from Japan's farming class. Most emigrated at the turn of the 19th century with the equivalent of an eighth grade education, although some were college educated. They had to contend with race prejudice and prohibitions that kept them from owning land, entering certain professions, and becoming naturalized citizens in the land where they raised their families.

Issei accepted jobs that called for hard labor and minimal knowledge of English. They worked on the railroads, in canneries, in logging camps, in mines, and on fishing boats. Agriculture offered the greatest opportunity for success. An immigrant could start as an ordinary laborer and progress to contract farming. Although some Japanese Americans bought farmland before the Alien Land Acts of 1913 and 1920 prohibited Asian land ownership, the best most Japanese Americans could hope for was to make a living by tenant sharing and leasing farmland. The majority of Japanese immigrants on the West Coast worked on farms, many as migrant laborers. By 1940, nearly half of the agricultural labor force on the West Coast was Japanese.

Those Japanese immigrants who lived in American cities usually worked as "houseboys," or domestics, for white families. Other Issei opened small businesses, such as dry goods stores, cafes, dry cleaners, laundries, grocery stores, and barbershops.

Anti-Asian sentiment kept the Japanese in America segregated in many ways. They developed their own network to finance Japanese businesses and to provide necessary services. California even established a separate school system for Japanese children. Discrimination against the Japanese kept trained professionals, such as doctors, from practicing outside the Japanese-American community, so the immigrants created separate health-care facilities. Although the Japanese had little contact with anyone outside their ethnic group, many Issei gained prominence in the Japanese-American community by solving legal problems, finding housing, and welcoming new Japanese immigrants.

 *Coney island is the all-American setting for this 1925 group photograph of Nisei children.*

The Issei tolerated the problems created by segregation with the hope that their children, the Nisei, would not be affected by the discrimination their parents had faced. The Issei's hopes centered around their children's success. The importance of this hope was expressed in the phrase *kodomo no tame ni,* meaning "for the sake of the children." The Issei encouraged their children to complete their education because they viewed a college degree as a ticket to success. While encouraging Americanization, the Issei sent their children to special after-school classes that taught the Japanese language and Japanese values to keep their cultural heritage alive. Most Nisei, however, sought a transition from their parents' world into American society.

51

*I don't care what they do with the
Japs, so long as they don't send them
back here. A Jap is a Jap.*

General John DeWitt, Commander
of the Western Defense Area

Wartime Evacuation

Japan's attack on the United States Naval fleet at Pearl Harbor on December 7, 1941, resulted in a crisis for the entire Japanese-American community. Immediately after the attack, the FBI arrested 2,192 prominent Issei. The anti-Japanese sentiment that had simmered for years reached fanatical proportions. Exclusionist groups, politicians, and newspapers pressed for the removal of all residents of Japanese ancestry from the West Coast of the United States.

President Franklin Roosevelt gave in to political pressure and on February 19, 1942, issued Executive Order 9066, permitting the "evacuation" of all persons of Japanese descent from California, Washington, and Oregon. The government uprooted Japanese Americans on the American mainland and held them in internment camps scattered throughout the United States until the end of World War II. Hawaii took no such measures, although Japanese Americans made up more than one-third of the population. Despite the American declara-

53

tion of war against Germany and Italy, no action was taken against immigrants from either of these two ethnic groups.

In March 1942, General John DeWitt, then commander in charge of the Western Defense Area, ordered the evacuation of all Japanese persons from the western half of the three Pacific Coast states and the southern third of Arizona. The order affected more than 110,000 of the 126,000 Japanese living on the West Coast. Of this number, 70,000 were American citizens. General DeWitt's now famous statement before the House Naval Affairs Subcommittee summed up the attitude of many Americans against the Japanese:

It makes no difference whether a Japanese is theoretically a citizen. He is still a Japanese. Giving him a scrap of paper won't change him. I don't care what they do with the Japs so long as they don't send them back here. A Jap is a Jap.

Posters informed Japanese Americans of the government's evacuation order.

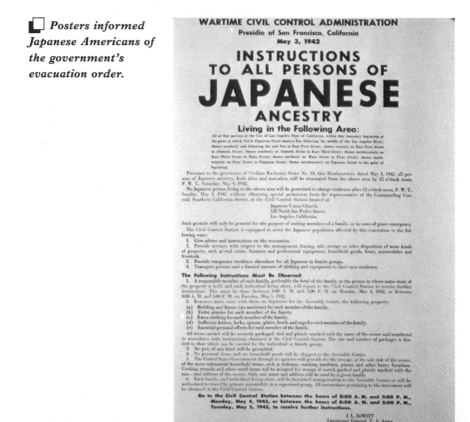

All evacuees had assembled at designated reporting centers, such as the Santa Anita Race Track, by August 7, 1942. Then, they took trains and buses to the camps that became their homes until the war ended. By November, these Japanese Americans had arrived at permanent camps in isolated desert areas of California, Arizona, Idaho, Utah, Wyoming, Colorado, and Arkansas.

For the most part, Japanese Americans responded voluntarily to the evacuation notices. Families could take only what they could carry. Many sold everything they owned within a few days or simply abandoned their belongings. Some stored possessions in government warehouses or left them with friends. Some lost personal treasures; others abandoned farms.

The process seemed quick and efficient, but some Japanese Americans refused to march peacefully to camp. Four legal cases challenging the government's right to imprison the Japanese eventually reached the United States Supreme Court. The cases, each brought by different individuals on

55

■ Japanese-American merchants declared their loyalty to America at the start of World War II.

■ The faces of Japanese Americans awaiting transportation to the detention camps show a mix of emotions.

different issues, were *Endo, Hirabayashi, Korematsu,* and *Yasui.* The day before the Supreme Court ruled in *Endo v. United States,* on December 17, 1944, the War Department announced that the Japanese could return home after January 2, 1945. The high court ruling in the *Endo* case found no legal basis for the indefinite detention of citizens of Japanese ancestry and proven loyalty. Despite the fears that encouraged the evacuation, no Japanese American was ever charged with disloyal acts against the United States government.

Life in the detention camps was strictly controlled. Barbed wire fences and towers with armed guards surrounded the camps. Housing consisted of military barracks or sometimes converted stables. Food was served in large

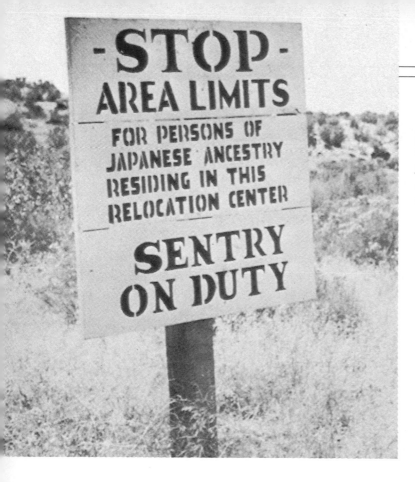

Boundary signs marked the limits of freedom for Japanese Americans in the detention camps.

mess halls. Family life disintegrated. Community leaders who had mediated disputes were among the first detained by the United States government. Most remained in a camp in Montana for some time before joining their families. Without their leadership, disputes sometimes erupted into violence. In some camps, riots, murders, and gang fights occurred.

The government permitted some Japanese Americans to leave the camps after they were cleared of being a threat to American security. Many evacuees applied for this permission and more than 35,000, mostly Nisei, had left the camps by 1943. Because they could not return to the West Coast, many went to live in the Midwest and the East. Some rejoined their families on the West Coast after the relocation centers closed.

"It Can't Be Helped"

Despite the hardships, most evacuees tried to maintain a normal life. They used the time to develop artistic skills or to further their education. Many attended high school and socialized at community dances, athletic contests, and other recreational activities. Although a normal lifestyle was not possible for the evacuees, their struggle to adjust was aided by a fatalistic point of view that stemmed from traditional Japanese religious beliefs. The Japanese phrase *shi-ka-ta-ga nai*, meaning "it can't be helped," characterizes this viewpoint.

In Canada the situation was even worse. The Canadian government entered World War II in 1939. In January 1942, it enacted the War Measures Act, calling for the placement of Japanese Canadians and Japanese aliens in detention camps. Canadian detention camps were located 100 miles inland

Men collected wood to keep the stoves burning at this Idaho camp.

FUJIHARA

from the western coast of British Columbia. Most of the camps were old, deserted mining towns. Families could not stay together. Men went to separate facilities in northern Ontario where they worked for $1 a day.

The Canadian government forced its Japanese residents held in these detention camps to pay for their limited housing from their savings. When they ran out of money, they had to work to pay for their board. Those who objected to the incarceration went, along with German prisoners from captured U-boats, into prisoner of war camps located in Northern Ontario.

Nisei Go to War

While most American men reported for military service in 1942, the Nisei living on the American mainland could not be drafted or accepted into military service if they volunteered. Their Selective Service classification was IV-C—meaning not acceptable for military service because of ancestry. Many Japanese Americans, however, were anxious to prove their loyalty by serving in the military.

After some prodding from Japanese civil rights organizations, an all-Nisei army group—the 442d Regimental Combat Team—was formed in January 1943. The unit absorbed Hawaii's 100th Battalion, which was made up of Japanese Americans who had been inducted into the army before Pearl Harbor was attacked. These Japanese-American soldiers received great public attention for their valor throughout Europe and in the Pacific. The men of the 442d won more than 3,600 Purple Hearts, 810 Bronze Stars, 342

In 1943, the military started accepting American-born Japanese.

Silver Stars, 47 Distinguished Service Crosses, and 6 distinguished unit citations, making the unit the most decorated in military history. The dedication and patriotism of the men of the 442d did much to change attitudes toward Japanese Americans.

A Changing World

The war changed traditional roles for the Japanese Americans as well as for other ethnic groups. Perhaps the most drastic change was in the role of women. Several hundred young Nisei women had joined the Women's Army Corps during World War II. And, like other American women, they had worked in defense plants, on railroads, and in mines, filling jobs left open by men who had gone to fight the war.

Many things also changed for the Japanese-American men after World War II. A California produce firm took a survey of its employees in 1942 and found 120 college-trained Japanese men working as clerks in its stores. By the late 1950s, the same schools that had barred Japanese as students were hiring the Nisei as teachers.

The Nisei experienced the same conflicts as did the children of all immigrants. They wanted to retain their parents' cultural heritage, but they also wanted to become part of the American mainstream. Responding to society's prejudices, they took refuge in their families and their ethnic community.

A turnaround in legislation affecting the Nisei's assimilation began in 1948 when the California courts overturned a law banning interracial marriage. In 1967, the United States Supreme Court in *Loving v. Virginia* ruled that all state laws banning interracial marriage (called antimiscegenation laws) were unconstitutional.

Hawaii's acceptance as the 50th state of the Union in 1960 marked another milestone in the Nisei's coming of age in American society. Hawaii became the first American state to elect public officials of Japanese ancestry on a large scale. The election sent Daniel Inouye and Spark Matsunaga, both sons of Issei immigrants, to the United States Senate. George Ariyoshi, also the son of Issei immigrants, became governor of Hawaii in 1974. But, on the whole, progress in social and recreational areas was slow for the Nisei.

 *New housing for elderly Japanese Americans replaces old homes in Los Angeles' Little Tokyo.*

Some prestigious, powerful social clubs remained closed to them, and housing discrimination did not erode until the 1960s.

Grandchildren of the Immigrants

The Sansei, children of the Nisei, are the most Americanized of the three generations. Most of them have gained acceptance in society, and they pursue higher education in impressive numbers. Despite the Sansei's assimilation of American values and lifestyles, they retain some distinguishing characteristics. Many prefer to join organizations such as fraternities and sororities with all-Asian memberships, so all-Japanese athletic leagues developed by the Nisei also continue to flourish.

The world of the Japanese American has changed so drastically within one generation that many Sansei question their parents' acceptance of the wartime evacuation. George Imai, the former president of the Japanese

Canadian Citizens Association, related the response the Nisei give their children: "We live for the future. We don't live for the past. Our philosophy has always been to conquer these problems—to learn from them."

Immigrants Today

According to the 1980 Census, the two most common occupations for Japanese-American men are technical sales and professional specialty jobs. Women work in the same fields as men but also work in clerical jobs. An increasing number of Sansei women work in occupations once considered "closed" to Asians: advertising, administration, the performing arts, and mass media.

The census also revealed that more than 700,000 Japanese Americans resided in the United States in 1980. Slightly more Japanese-American women than men made up this ethnic group. Their median age was 33.6 years, and family size averaged 3.26. More than 90 percent lived in urban areas. The majority of Japanese Americans lived in the western states, while the northeast, north central, and southern states each claimed approximately 7 percent of the Japanese-American population. Almost 70 percent of persons of Japanese ancestry residing in the United States were born here.

By 1981, almost 41,000 Japanese resided in Canada. Ontario and British Columbia had the largest Japanese population. More than 16,000 Japanese Canadians lived in each of these two provinces. Only 1,395 Japanese lived in Quebec, and only 40 Japanese Canadians lived in Nova Scotia.

Tradition and Transition

Some Japanese traditions, especially festivals, give Japanese Americans the chance to keep ancient customs alive. The first Japanese immigrants left a country in which festivals were celebrated throughout the year. Most of these festivals related to the changing seasons and were observed in the cities as well as in country villages. Four ancient festivals—New Year's (O-Shogatsu), the Buddhist Festival of the Dead (O-Bon), Girls' Day (Hinamatsuri), and Boys' Day (Tango-no-sekku)—continue to be observed.

The Japanese New Year, O-Shogatsu, is a happy occasion celebrated for three days—unlike the American tradition of one night of fun to welcome the New Year. One of the traditions of O-Shogatsu that still thrives is eating *mochi*, a rice cake.

Preparing mochi was a long and arduous process. Men traditionally took the first step in preparing mochi by pounding the rice into a thick paste. Women then put the paste on a board and molded it into flat balls. Like

65

many ancient customs, this time-consuming recipe has been replaced in modern times with a store-bought alternative.

After a New Year's Eve supper of noodles, the head of the household may follow the ancient custom of placing a pair of bamboo reeds over the front door. The Japanese believe the reeds symbolize faithfulness in marriage and the family's ability to "bend and not break." The Japanese also

The tradition of pounding rice to make mochi has declined because store-bought products are more convenient.

believe that joy or sadness on New Year's is an omen for the remainder of the year. Therefore, they allow no unhappiness.

O Bon, the Festival of the Dead, is an ancient Buddhist tribute to Japanese ancestors. O-Bon is often called the Festival of the Lanterns, after the many lanterns that hang along the long porches of shrines and temples in Japan. The Festival of Lanterns is a celebration of birth and death for a

people whose ancient religion revolves around the spirit of dead family members. Today, the Issei keep this holiday alive by going to church and visiting ancestors' graves. They clear the graves of weeds and debris and place flowers on them. Traditionally, family members placed food on the graves and considered it good luck for children to eat the various fruits and candies they found in the cemeteries.

Two Japanese holidays honor children: Hinamatsuri, or Girls' Day, on March 3, is a festival of dolls. On this festival, young girls decorate their dolls and hold a tea party in their honor. The girls dress in their very best clothes and visit the homes of young friends. Tango-no-sekku, Boys' Day, on May 5, is a celebration honoring the strength of the sons in Japanese families. Families usually fly cotton carp flags on bamboo poles outside their homes. (To the Japanese, the carp is a symbol of courage and endurance.) One carp flag is usually flown for each son in the family.

Japanese-American Food

Americans are familiar with the term *sushi*—but most mistakenly believe it means "raw fish." Actually, sushi means "with rice." Sushi rice is usually

■ *On Girls' Day, these youngsters hold a tea party for their dolls.*

■ *To celebrate Boys' Day, Japanese families fly one carp flag for each son. The carp is a symbol of courage and endurance.*

made with vinegar. *Sashimi*, the most popular form of raw fish, is made with slices of octopus, tuna, and flounder and is only one of the many side dishes that may accompany sushi.

Sukiyaki is made from strips of beef, vegetables, bean curd, and noodles, all cooked quickly in a sauce made from sugar and soybeans. In Japanese restaurants throughout America, diners enjoy watching chefs prepare this dish. The quickness of the chef's hands as he slices the meal's ingredients amazes most Westerners.

Another popular Japanese dish is *tempura*, which consists of seafood or vegetables dipped in batter and fried in deep fat. *Sake*, the delicious rice wine usually served hot in small porcelain cups, is drunk with meals in traditional Japanese households. In a modern variation, it is poured over ice for a refreshing summer drink.

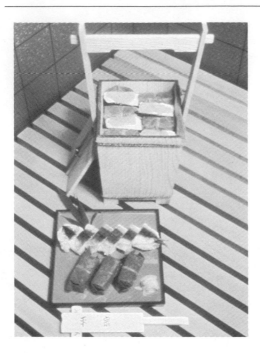

■ *The typical Japanese sashimi dinner features slices of raw fish, such as octopus or tuna, as a main ingredient.*

■ *Seafood and vegetables are dipped in batter and deep fried to make tempura.*

Traditional Costume

Sometimes, Hollywood movies show Japanese people wearing *kimonos* and removing their shoes when they enter a home. Some Japanese still practice these traditions. Both men and women often wear the kimono, a long robe with wide sleeves and a broad sash (called an *obi*), on New Year's and other holidays. Most Japanese girls wear kimonos on Girls' Day. In Japan, the traditional robe is worn at weddings and funerals. Few Japanese today follow the ancient Buddhist tradition of removing their shoes before they enter a home, but it is still observed when the floor is covered with a heavy straw mat called a *tatami.*

71

Even the realities of World War II
could not deter Japanese Americans
from realizing their share of the
American Dream.

Japanese-American Contributions

When the first Japanese immigrants arrived in 1890, certain Issei broke barriers of prejudice and brought respect to their ethnic group. By educating themselves and overcoming discrimination, Japanese Americans have revealed immense talents throughout the 20th century. Their achievements are those of a people who have fought the odds and triumphed.

Two Issei who distinguished themselves in science during the 19th century were Hideyo Noguchi and Jokichi Takamine. Noguchi (1876-1928) arrived in America in 1899 to work in the pathology lab at the University of Pennsylvania. Noted for his research in the study of yellow fever and syphilis, he was also well respected for his studies of snake venom. Ironically, Noguchi died of yellow fever while studying the disease in Africa. His birthplace in Inawashiro, Japan, is now a shrine to his memory.

Jokichi Takamine (1854-1922) was raised in the tradition of the samurai, but later decided on a career in

73

■ *Japanese scientist Hideyo Noguchi was noted for his research on yellow fever.*

■ *Dr. Jokichi Takamine was both a noted chemist and a philanthropist.*

chemistry. Takamine arrived in the United States in 1884 and began working to isolate adrenalin—the first gland hormone to be discovered in pure form. The founder of the Japanese Association of New York, Takamine was a philanthropist who helped other Issei, especially those in the fields of chemistry, art, and music.

In 1985, Ellison Onizuka became the first descendant of Japanese immigrants to fly in space. Born in 1946, he spent most of his childhood watching the stars through a telescope at Honolulu's Bishop Museum. After studying aerospace engineering at the University of Colorado, he spent eight years as an Air Force test pilot and flight engineer. He joined the National Aeronautics and Space Administration (NASA) as an astronaut candidate in 1978. He was a mission specialist on the classified military flight of the space shuttle Discovery in 1985. Onizuka was a member of the crew of the tragic flight of the space shuttle Challenger that exploded in 1986, killing the seven astronauts aboard.

Political Contributions

George Ryochi Ariyoshi was the first American of Japanese ancestry to become a state governor. Ariyoshi was born on March 12, 1926, the son of a

Ellison Onizuka was the first Japanese American to fly in space.

sumo wrestler. He received his law degree from the University of Michigan in 1953. After practicing criminal law, he began his political career with a successful bid for a seat in Hawaii's House of Representatives. He became lieutenant governor of Hawaii in 1970. Ariyoshi took office as governor of Hawaii in 1974 and served three consecutive terms.

Soon after Hawaii became the 50th state, Dan Ken Inouye was elected the first Japanese-American congressman. Born on September 7, 1924, he enlisted as a private in the famed 442d Regimental Combat Team during World War II. By the time Captain Inouye was discharged in 1947, he had lost an arm in combat. Because of this loss, he decided on a career in law instead of pursuing a medical career as he had intended. In 1952, he received his law degree from George Washington University. Inouye was sworn in as a congressman on August 24, 1959, and joined the Banking and Currency Committee. In 1963, Inouye became a member of the United States Senate and has held that position ever since.

When Inouye became a senator, he was succeeded in the House of Representatives by Spark Matsunaga, another former member of the Nisei 442d Infantry. Matsunaga also served in the Hawaiian 100th battalion. Reelected four times to the House of Representatives, he now serves as a United States senator.

Patsy Takemoto Mink, Hawaii's first Nisei woman lawyer, became a representative to Congress in 1964. She received her law degree from the University of Chicago in 1951. Reelected to three congressional terms, she has served on the Interior and Insular Affairs Committee as well as the Education and Labor Committee.

Senator Samuel Ichiye Hayakawa, born July 18, 1906, in Vancouver, British Columbia, is one of the most colorful political figures to emerge from the 1970s. After receiving his Ph.D. in English from the University of Wisconsin, Hayakawa became a renowned scholar in linguistics. Books such as *Language in Action* (1941) and *Symbol, Status and Personality* (1963) established him as a best-selling author. When he was appointed president of San Francisco State College in 1968, he became the first Japanese American to hold such a position. Hayakawa gained national attention when he confronted student demonstrators in 1968. He left his college presidency in

■ *Dan Ken Inouye, the first Japanese American elected to congress, has represented Hawaii in the United States Senate since 1963.*

1973 and campaigned successfully for a seat as senator from California. He served in the United States Senate from 1977 to 1981.

Architecture and Art

Japanese Americans have achieved prominence in the fields of architecture and art. One of these is architect Minoru Yamasaki (1912-1986), a Nisei born in Seattle, Washington. Perhaps his greatest legacy is the World Trade Center, which he designed for the Port Authority of New York. The center's twin towers are the world's second-tallest buildings. Yamasaki's modernist work includes more than 300 designs, including Los Angeles's Western Century Plaza Hotel and Tower, the Federal Science Pavilion at Seattle's Century 21 Exposition, and the Dhahran Airport in Saudi Arabia. He once described his work as consisting of "delight, serenity, and surprise."

Isamu Noguchi has a worldwide reputation as a sculptor. Born in Los Angeles in 1904 to an American mother and a Japanese father, he spent his childhood in Japan. Abandoning a career in medicine, he received a Guggenheim Fellowship to study art in 1927. He worked for two years in Paris as an assistant to the abstract sculptor Constantin Brancusi. When he returned to Japan, Noguchi studied landscapes and the use of natural materials in art. In 1935, he became interested in theater and ballet and began designing stage sets. His most famous publicly-displayed sculpture is the 28-foot-high, bright red cube that stands on one point in front of the Marine Midland Grace Trust Company in New York City.

Sculptor Isamu Noguchi's "Red Cube" balances precariously in front of the Marine Midland Grace Trust Company in New York City.

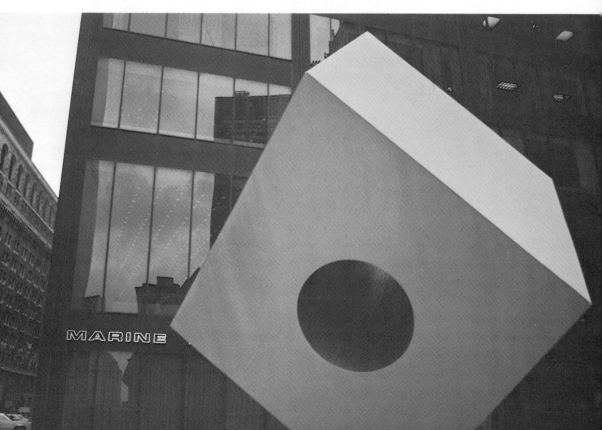

 *Seiji Ozawa is director of the Boston Symphony Orchestra.*

Musical Accomplishments

Seiji Ozawa, born September 1, 1935, in Hoten, Japan, was the first Japanese orchestra conductor to achieve fame in the Western world. Although he had planned a career as a concert pianist, he decided to become a conductor after he broke both index fingers in a soccer accident at the age of 19. Praised by the great American composer Aaron Copeland, Ozawa came to the attention of Leonard Bernstein. Under this guidance, he took a position as assistant conductor of the New York Philharmonic.

Ozawa returned to Japan as the musical director of Tokyo's Nisei Theatre in 1963. In Tokyo, he broadened his scope to include work with the opera company. In 1965, he began a three-year tenure as conductor of the Toronto Symphony Orchestra, followed by a five-year stint with the San Francisco Symphony. Since 1973, his position as director of the Boston Symphony Orchestra has brought him worldwide attention.

Jazz musician Toshiko Akiyoshi was born December 12, 1929, in Dairen, Manchuria. At the end of World War II, she was a Japanese teenager

Sessue Hayakawa won acclaim for his role in **Bridge On the River Kwai.**

whose family could not afford a piano. "I started to play in a dance hall," she recalls, "and my father almost disowned me." After pursuing a career as a jazz pianist in Tokyo, Akiyoshi entered the Berkeley School of Music in Boston in 1956. A band leader, arranger, and composer, she is one of the most acclaimed women in jazz. In 1967, she had her own radio show in New York. She made her debut at Carnegie Hall in 1971. Akiyoshi sees her music as "a reflection of my thoughts in a jazz language."

Television and Movies

Film actor Sessue Hayakawa (1889-1973) was born in Chiba, Japan, and immigrated to the United States shortly before World War I. He achieved his greatest fame for his portrayal of the commandant of the prisoner of war camp in *The Bridge On the River Kwai,* a role that won him an Oscar nomination in 1957. Hayakawa studied political science and drama at the University of Chicago and began his film career in 1914 with the silent film *The Typhoon.* During the next few decades, he made many films, including *Daughter of the Dragon* (1931) and *Tokyo Joe* (1949).

Miyoshi Umeki, born in 1929, is one of the few Japanese-American women to receive national recognition. Her film roles are familiar to many Americans. She won the Academy Award for best supporting actress for her work in the 1957 film *Sayonara,* in which she starred with Red Buttons and Marlon Brando. After appearing in other movies, including the popular *Flower Drum Song* (1961), she became known to American television audiences for her portrayal of the endearing Mrs. Livingston on "The Courtship of Eddie's Father."

Actor Jack Soo (1915-1979) is best remembered for his role as Nick Yemana on television's "Barney Miller." Born Goro Suzuki, the actor changed his name after being interned during World War II at Camp Topaz in Utah. During his long career, he appeared in many movies, including *Flower Drug Song* (1961), *Thoroughly Modern Millie* (1967), and *Green Berets* (1968).

Another actor whose face is familiar to the American public is Noriyuki "Pat" Morita. In *The Karate Kid,* a movie released in 1984, Morita played an apartment complex handyman who taught martial arts and Confucian wisdom to a teenager challenged by high school classmates. For his performance, Morita received an Academy Award nomination for best supporting actor. He revived the role in 1986 for a sequel, *The Karate Kid Part II.* (Morita is pictured on page 72.)

The son of immigrant migrant farm workers, Morita was born in 1932 and spent much of his childhood recovering from spinal tuberculosis at a sanatorium near Sacramento, California. While Morita was at the sanatorium, an Irish priest who befriended him gave him the nickname "Pat." When he recovered at the age of 11, Morita was taken to join his parents at the Manzanar internment camp in California. He began his show business career as a stand-up comedian, but gained national attention for his role as Arnold on the hit television series "Happy Days."

East Meets West

As different as the Japanese seemed to Americans when they first arrived in the United States, their way of looking at the world was very similar to that of the American pioneers. The Japanese work ethic of personal discipline, deference to authority, high productivity, and emphasis on quality is very similar to the Protestant work ethic that the Pilgrims brought to America. Therefore, the Japanese adjusted well to the American marketplace.

The Japanese were late arrivals in the massive wave of immigration to the United States. Japanese were ineligible for citizenship. They could not own land in California, and their children attended segregated schools. Yet, by the 1960s, the personal income of Japanese Americans was 11 percent higher than the national average. Their average family income was 32 percent higher.

Japanese Americans learned early that education would move them up the social ladder and encouraged their children to attain an education. By 1981, more than half of the third generation of Japanese Americans (Sansei) were attending college. Another factor that aided assimilation was the fact that Japanese culture is so agreeable to Americans. Japanese art, food, architecture, and even flower arranging and gardening have become an integral part of American life. In Japanese Americans, East meets West.

Today, Japanese culture is part of the American mainstream. Students study and write haiku poetry. Many adults find a peaceful refuge in the meditative process of Zen Buddhism. Others practice martial arts such as judo, which has become an Olympic sport.

The economies of Japan and the United States are becoming more and more dependent on each other as American industry begins to accept Japanese technical innovations. Through these advancements, the Western world is learning how similar the two cultures are.

Traditional Japanese culture encouraged harmony. This heritage enabled Japanese Americans to withstand years of discrimination. But they have not hesitated to stand up for their rights. As early as 1916, individual Japanese Americans openly challenged the laws that kept them from becoming naturalized citizens. The U.S. Supreme Court heard two cases involving

Like the majority of Sansei, these third-generation Japanese Americans are attending college.

85

this issue while the United States was fighting World War I. After that war, Japanese Americans pushed for legislation to allow those Japanese Americans who served in the military to become naturalized citizens. Congress passed special legislation in response to this lobbying effort, permitting 700 Japanese veterans of World War I to become naturalized American citizens.

The younger generations of Japanese Americans have protested the World War II incarceration of their parents and grandparents. Five Sansei attorneys offered a legal brief in 1980 outlining the constitutional violations involved in the internment camps. These attorneys, along with dozens of volunteer lawyers and law students, convinced the U.S. Supreme Court to

Bill Kochiyama gives emotional testimony at a federal hearing on Japanese internment.

☐ *An internment survivor, Karl Akiya, displays a poster during a program commemorating the internment.*

CORKY LEE

reopen a case that had resulted in the convictions of three Japanese Americans who protested the internment during the 1940s. The court overturned the convictions in 1983. In addition, Congress established a special commission to investigate the circumstances that led to Roosevelt's Executive Order 9066. Hundreds of Japanese Americans testified at the 1981 hearings before the United States Commission on Wartime Relocation and Internment of Civilians. The commission concluded that the order was not justified by military necessity and that it had done "a grave injustice" to the more than 100,000 Japanese Americans interned during the war.

Representative Jim Wright, a Democrat from Texas and the House majority leader, introduced a bill in 1985 to compensate wartime evacuees for their losses. More than 100 lawmakers supported Wright's bill calling for a $1.5 billion fund that would compensate each of the 60,000 remaining survivors of the internment camps with a compensatory payment of $20,000. The bill has not yet been passed, and as the national budget tightens, funding the plan remains a problem. In Canada, a similar bill has been introduced in the Canadian Parliament. However, this bill does not call for individual recompensation.

Japanese Americans survived the detention camps with the firm belief that their share of the American dream would return. They were right. This is the lesson of their brave perseverance and spiritual acceptance of their fate. The grandchildren of the immigrants acknowledge their elders' endurance and sacrifice. Astronaut Ellison Onizuka offered these thoughts on that sacrifice after his first spaceflight:

> I looked down as we passed over Hawaii and thought about all the sacrifices of all the people who helped me along the way. My grandparents, who were contract laborers; my parents, who did without to send me to college; my school teachers, coaches, and ministers—all the past generations who pulled together to create the present. Different people, different races, different religions—all working toward a common goal, all one family.

It was the sacrifices made by Onizuka's grandparents and the thousands like them that allowed these Japanese Americans to create a bright future for their children and grandchildren. They had faith in the democratic way of life and in their new country. Japanese Americans overcame the obstacles to become a viable part of American society.

Selected References

Bloom, Leonard, and Riemer, Ruth. "Attitudes of College Students Toward Japanese Americans." *Sociometry* 8 (May 1945).

Eaton, Allen H. *Beauty Behind Barbed Wire*. New York: Harper & Brothers, 1952.

Irons, Peter. *Justice at War*. New York: Oxford University Press, 1983.

Kitano, Harry. "Japanese Americans: the Development of a Middleman Minority?" *Pacific Historical Review* 43 (April 1974): 500-19.

Melendy, H. Brett. *The Oriental Americans*. Boston: Twayne Publishers, a Division of G.K. Hall & Co., 1972.

Ogawa, Dennis. *Kodomo No Tame Ni: For the Sake of the Children*. Honolulu: University of Hawaii Press, 1978.

Smith, Bradford. *Americans From Japan*. Philadelphia: J.B. Lippincott Co., 1948.

Strong, Edward. *The Second Generation Japanese Problem*. Stanford: Stanford University Press, 1934.

Thomas, Dorothy, and Nishimoto, Richard. *The Spoilage*. Berkeley: University of California Press, 1946.

U.S. Congress. House. *Report of Commission on Wartime Relocation and Internment of Civilians*. Washington, D.C.: U.S. Government Printing Office, 1982.

Index